SUN SIGN SECRETS

SAGITTARIUS

22 NOVEMBER — 21 DECEMBER

SUN SIGN SECRETS

SAGITTARIUS

22 NOVEMBER — 21 DECEMBER

BERNARD FITZWALTER

AQUARIAN

THE AQUARIAN PRESS

First published 1989

British Library Cataloguing in Publication Data

Fitzwalter, Bernard
Sun sign secrets : Sagittarius.
1. Signs of the zodiac
I. Title
133.5′2

ISBN 0-85030-694-9

The Aquarian Press is part of the
Thorsons Publishing Group,
Wellingborough, Northamptonshire,
NN8 2RQ, England

Printed in Great Britain by Cox and Wyman Limited,
Reading, Berkshire

1 3 5 7 9 10 8 6 4 2

CONTENTS

Bernard Fitzwalter.

INTRODUCTION

People love finding out about themselves through astrology, and the two questions which are asked most frequently are 'What am I like?' and 'Who is best suited to me?' This little book will answer both of those questions, and it will answer a lot more as well. It will identify not only the person best suited to you, but also the person you are most likely to disagree with — and every possible variation in between.

And there's more. Most people are obsessed with their appearance, but few have any idea that their zodiac sign has any bearing on the way they look. It has, and here's a special guide to help you match the signs to physique. Cars . . . holidays . . . favourite food . . . The list goes on and on, yet the zodiac touches all of these and more, making everything reflect your birthday. It's all laid out here for you, along with everything else you could want to know about *your* sign, from the famous people born under it to the myth which lies behind it.

Dip in, and get to know yourself!

The typical Sagittarius!

BEING A SAGITTARIUS

A famous astrologer of the 1930s, asked which sign they'd like to be, given the choice, replied 'Sagittarius!'. The luckiest sign by far, its natives never worry, and never need to. You have flair, talent, imagination, and the ability to come out of the tightest scrapes sunny side up and smiling. How do you do it?

It's all because of the influence, through your sign, of the planet Jupiter. You Sagittarians are big people, even when you're small (which isn't often!). You are big-hearted, big-boned, and have big ideas. You are also big spenders and sometimes big-headed, but it doesn't seem to matter. This is because each and every one of you is full of the energy of the planet Jupiter, the biggest planet in the solar system. Jupiter gives us the word 'jovial': there is something about his influence that makes us smile, no matter what.

Jupiter is essentially good-natured, but he gets everywhere, and so does the Sagittarian. You have an insatiable curiosity about things, and would dearly love to know all there is to know about everything. To you, knowing things, and finding out more things to know, is fun. It never occurs to you that some things might be dangerous to know, dangerous to find out, or dangerous to tell people that you know; as far as you're concerned, knowledge is free for all to find and use, and you will tell anybody anything. Whatever your friends confide in you, you will tell to anyone else who asks; whatever occurs to you when you see somebody, you tell them straight, without ever thinking that they might not care to know. This openness and honesty (for that's all it is) gets you a reputation for tactlessness and gossiping which you feel is undeserved. In a way, it is; the inference is that you are in some way malicious, whereas the truth is that there is nobody in the zodiac more honest and fair than the Sagittarian. There is no reason for you to be dishonest, anyway; you don't even have to try to win if Jupiter is behind you.

Sagittarians are excited by the prospect of anything new, especially if it comes from far away. The romance of travel for its own sake is particularly yours; you can't think of anything worse than living in the same place for the rest of your life, and you can't think of anything better than a train ticket to Istanbul offered by a dark stranger. You know that the more things you see, the more things there will be to see, and you also know that you'll get through it all without serious mishap. Staying still, putting down roots and building a cosy family life sounds dreadful to an adventurer like you; new people and new experiences are what you long for.

There are two basic sorts of Sagittarians, and anybody who has ever attempted to tidy your bedroom will be able to tell you which one you are, if you don't already know. First are the intellectual sorts, who read books on anything and everything. Novels, travel, history, anything at all. If you are one of these, you can never pass a bookshop without going in and buying at least three, often on subjects that you had never thought of until you saw the book in the shop. You are probably good at languages; you are the sort who can learn a language from the waiters on holiday.

The second sort of Sagittarian is the sporty and active sort. If it involves movement, you do it. Riding, skiing, and all motorized sports appeal, because they get you there faster, and that's what you really enjoy, isn't it? You probably have a vast collection of bags; the reason is that you keep thinking that you will need them to put things in when you next travel somewhere, which would ideally be at a moment's notice. Depressed Sagittarians are usually to be found buying bags or maps, or thumbing through travel brochures — the very idea of going somewhere cheers you up.

Despite Jupiter's influence and help, you do have one or two faults, but somehow everyone tends not to notice them. One of the biggest is your inability to see anything on a small scale; you're full of grand ideas and wonderful schemes, but the little details that make them work are too small for you to grasp, and you make mistakes. Spending time with fiddly things annoys you — you're impatient to be finished and on to the next thing, and as you wrestle with a jammed lock on a suitcase, or a faulty telephone, your patience evaporates almost at once. Rather than take your time, you're more likely to leave it behind or do without it altogether.

The same thing happens at work, too. You can see the principles and the eventual aim of the job at once, but the details which have to be learned so that it is performed properly don't interest you, and although you ought to be able to master them with your eyes closed, almost, you make silly slips because you have become bored. Your carelessness doesn't count against you, though, because most people don't mind the odd error here and there — in fact they prefer you like that to someone who gets everything right and is always perfect. Virgos, who are good at detail but very poor at seeing the larger view, are much less popular than Sagittarians, so it appears that even your faults work to your advantage. There's Sagittarianism for you.

The greatest quality that you have is optimism. It never really crosses your mind that things won't turn out well in the end; 'happily ever after' is a statement of fact to you, whereas the other eleven signs know that only fairy tales end like that. Whenever you are down, or squeeze, you can always find something to catch your attention and lift your spirits, and more often than not use it to provide a solution to your difficulties. This requires more than mere chance, it requires a lifelong, never-failing streak of pure luck, and Sagittarians have exactly that in the form of Jupiter, which never lets you down. Knowing that you will always manage, somehow, means that you get to be more careless with yourself and your efforts than you might be, whereas other signs work hard and save their earnings for rainy days.

That same optimism applies to your personal relationships, too. When you're in love, you give your partner everything you've got, like a big, boisterous puppy, and it's sometimes a bit much for the other person to take. It's not that they don't like you, but your enthusiasm is rather overwhelming, especially in the first stages of a relationship.

Sagittarians aren't the most constant lovers. Anything new is interesting to you for that very reason, and so a new person is always more interesting than someone you already know, no matter how close you are. Sagittarian optimism always says that the next person will be even better — and even when that proves not to be true, you know that the *next* one will be, and so on. It also never occurs to you that the ones you leave behind you are at all upset; you didn't mean to hurt them, after all, and you don't feel upset yourself, so why should they?

As you can see, you can be a bit naive about emotions at times. This is because you don't need anyone else as an emotional support, thanks to Jupiter. Nor do you want anyone to be dependent on you; you like the freedom to chase after new ideas, new people and new places. What you're really after is someone who likes your company as much as you like theirs, and who is with you because they think it's fun. People like this are hard to find, but you'll keep looking — and with your luck, you'll probably find them.

Quiz: How Sagittarian Are You?

Here's a simple way to find out how close to being the textbook Sagittarian you are. There are two sets of questions, Section A and Section B. Just choose the answer which seems closest to the way you feel or would act in that situation, and check your score at the end.

Section A?

1. If you met an intruder in your garden one night, would you
- (a) have a go at him?
- (b) tell him it was your garden and would he please leave?
- (c) try to reason with him?
- (d) run away or hide?

2. When you go to the movies, do you choose
- (a) an all-action picture with a dynamic hero?
- (b) something glamorous and easy on the eye?
- (c) a film with a message, maybe a foreign language film?
- (d) a love story or a weepie?

3. What appeals to you most in a person of the opposite sex?
- (a) Their body.

(b)　Their lifestyle.
(c)　Their lively conversation.
(d)　Their kindness and concern.

4. What do you want out of a job?
(a)　Excitement and challenge.
(b)　Power, responsibility, and money.
(c)　Variety and interesting people.
(d)　Security

5. When talking to somebody new, are you
(a)　honest and open, saying anything you feel like?
(b)　keen that they should form a good impression of you?
(c)　happy to embroider the truth a little as you go along, to keep the conversation sparkling?
(d)　shy and reserved, letting slip very little about yourself?

6. What do you like to do with your money?
(a)　Spend it on outrageous and amusing things for yourself.
(b)　Spend it on quality possessions which will last.
(c)　Spend it on your friends, on socializing, and on holidays.
(d)　Save it, in case you need it for anything.

7. How do you see children?
(a)　Good, boisterous fun.
(b)　The future of your family, a responsibility but a bit noisy.
(c)　Lively, talkative, amusing companions.
(d)　Endearing souls who need your love and care.

8. How would you describe your style of dress?
(a)　Dynamic.
(b)　Classic.

(c) Informal.
(d) Romantic/Seductive.

9. Which of these would you most like to live in?
(a) A villa in Italy or the South of France.
(b) An eight-bedroomed mansion with a gravel drive, tennis courts and a swimming pool.
(c) A Manhattan penthouse with a fabulous view of New York.
(d) A lovely little cottage by the waterside.

10. If your fairy godmother gave you a wish, would you choose
(a) lifelong fame?
(b) lifelong wealth?
(c) to be clever, witty, and popular?
(d) to have true love for ever?

SECTION B

1. If you inherited a country house in some disrepair, would you
(a) make plans to fix it and extend it with new additions of your own?
(b) restore it to its former glory and maintain it in that condition?
(c) convert it into something else, like an hotel or a conference centre?

2. It's your first day in a new job. Do you
(a) do it the way you think best?
(b) find out how your predecessor did things, and copy his way of working?
(c) ask around, establish communication, see what was wrong before, and what you can bring to the problem now?

3. Would you rather
   (a) make things?
   (b) buy things?
   (c) sell things?

4. On arrival at your holiday destination you find that your hotel room is double-booked. Do you
   (a) Complain, arrange a full refund on the spot, and march off to see if any of the other hotels in town have anything suitable?
   (b) Stay where you are and refuse to move until you get your room?
   (c) Try to come to an arrangement with the management, taking a smaller room and some financial compensation as well?

5. Which of these do you find the most attractive quality in a person?
   (a) Initiative.
   (b) Reliability.
   (c) Tolerance.

6. What kind of career are you aiming for?
   (a) Something where you can get to the top.
   (b) Something stable and secure, where you can make steady progress until you get your pension.
   (c) Nothing, really just a series of different jobs which you take as the interest and opportunity arise.

7. Is your dream car
   (a) A pure performance car, not necessarily reliable or practical?
   (b) A head-turning limousine with every possible refinement?
   (c) A truly versatile all-rounder, able to do everything well and to go anywhere with ease?

8. In making decisions, do you
  (a)   make instant judgements and stick to them?
  (b)   try not to be too hasty, and take the safe option?
  (c)   change your mind once or twice before reaching a final conclusion?

9. Some project you have worked on for a long time breaks down and collapses completely. Do you
  (a)   shrug your shoulders, then make a start on something different, without a backward glance?
  (b)   do whatever is necessary to repair it and rebuild it bit by bit, since total loss is unthinkable?
  (c)   see if any parts of it are worth salvaging and using in something else?

10. Think of your least attractive physical feature. Would you like it to be
  (a)   better?
  (b)   bigger?
  (c)   different?

How Did You Score?

If you chose mostly (a)s in Section A and mostly (a)s in Section B, then your responses are typical of an Aries.

If you chose mostly (a)s in Section A and mostly (b)s in Section B, then your responses are typical of a Leo.

If you chose mostly (a)s in Section A and mostly (c)s in Section B, then your responses are typical of a Sagittarius.

If you chose mostly (b)s in Section A and mostly (a)s in Section B, then your responses are typical of a Capricorn.

If you chose mostly (b)s in Section A and mostly (b)s in Section B, then your responses are typical of a Taurus.

If you chose mostly (b)s in Section A and mostly (c)s in Section B, then your responses are typical of a Virgo.

If you chose mostly (c)s in Section A and mostly (a)s in Section B, then your responses are typical of a Libra.

If you chose mostly (c)s in Section A and mostly (b)s in Section B, then your responses are typical of an Aquarius.

If you chose mostly (c)s in Section A and mostly (c)s in Section B, then your responses are typical of a Gemini.

If you chose mostly (d)s in Section A and mostly (a)s in Section B, then your responses are typical of a Cancer.

If you chose mostly (d)s in Section A and mostly (b)s in Section B, then your responses are typical of a Scorpio.

If you chose mostly (d)s in Section A and mostly (c)s in Section B, then your responses are typical of a Pisces.

Don't worry if you find that your responses belong to a different sign from your Sun sign. It doesn't mean that you have answered incorrectly, or that astrology is rubbish, or somebody has been telling you lies about when your birthday is. What it means is that your Sagittarius-ness is outweighed by other factors in your horoscope, such as the position of the Moon, or the rising sign (see page 40), which are probably in signs other than Sagittarius. This will make you think and react in the manner of the other signs, rather than in a Sagittarian way — it's part of what makes everybody unique.

THE SAGITTARIAN LIFESTYLE

HOME

Your home is probably a wonderful mess, full of muddy boots, things from foreign lands, and lots and lots of books. Your casual, rather untidy personal style transfers itself to your home quite easily, but the good thing about it is that nobody ever feels that they have to behave in a certain way when they come to visit. It's a place for people to be at ease in, and everyone feels comfortable the moment they arrive.

Your furniture is likely to be rather large, and quite hefty, because it has to withstand you throwing yourself around on it, and generally abusing it. Warm autumnal colours predominate, such as reds and browns; white and blue are too cool for your taste. You are far more likely to spend time in the kitchen than in a sitting room or bedroom; it's the most informal place in any house, and it's where you can do something about the immense appetite you bring home with you each time you return.

There will always be books, in every room, along with newspapers and magazines — kept because they have something in them which has excited your interest — and of course maps, which all Sagittarians love, because they remind you of travelling.

CARS

Sagittarians get a great deal of pleasure out of cars. You have the love of machinery and speed that your Fire sign colleagues the Arians have, and a love of travelling which is all your own; together they explain the way you feel about your car.

What you like best about your car is driving it. That may sound obvious, but the fact is that most of the other signs buy their cars for reasons other than the pleasure of driving them; only the Fire signs — Aries, Leo, and you, Sagittarius — put the experience of driving at the top of the list of things a car has to offer. And even the Leo would sometimes rather be chauffeured, so that just leaves you and the Arian.

What the Earth signs want, for example, is for the car to be comfortable, a sort of living room on wheels, where the smell of the leather seats and the whirr of the electric windows is more rewarding than actually driving it. Ask your Taurean or Capricornian friends (if you have any — see the diagram on p. 31) about their cars, and you'll soon see that the depth of the paint means more to them than the sound of the engine.

Water signs want security and anonymity; they see their car as a suit of armour which keeps them safe from the outside world. It's hard to imagine that as a principal consideration when buying a car, isn't it?

You see, you're such a purist. You don't need protecting, because you're so open and so optimistic. You don't need cosseting with material comforts either, because you'd rather be actively involved than sit still. You see the car in its purest sense, as a machine for travelling in.

The difference between you and the Arian is that he sees a car as a travelling *machine*, and you see it as a *travelling* machine. What matters most to him is the roar of the exhaust and how fast it goes, and though you like these too, your interest lies in how far it will take you.

The idea of distance is the key to understanding Sagittarian thought, and to your love of cars. Some people use cars for convenience, for going down to the shops, but long-legged Sagittarians can walk there just as quickly; what you buy your car for is to go adventuring, not shopping.

It doesn't really matter whether you regularly drive to Rome, or Vienna, or not; the essential thing is that you'd like to think that you could, and the idea of doing it has a tremendous appeal to you. You choose your car to represent the idea of going long distances, and to show that you are a person who loves travelling.

For these reasons you are unlikely to choose a small car, or a short one, given the choice. A small car, may be all that you can afford at the moment, or maybe your car comes with your job, but if you were given the choice, your eye would be drawn to something rather longer or larger than the average familiy hatchback. Size is an important consideration: people with big ideas and big personalities choose big cars, and a Sagittarian's ideas are bigger than almost anybody else's. Similarly, Sagittarians are usually tall, and long in the leg, which all ties in with the idea of travelling long distances, of course, and so you choose a car which is long in the leg too; the long and elegant lines of a Jaguar, say, are much more appealing to you than, for example, the rather rounder outline of a Granada.

All the virtues of a small car, such as its nippiness, economy, and the lightness of its controls, are lost on you, because your imagination always see the far horizon as the goal rather than practical details. What you eventually buy is probably far too large and cumbersome for dense city traffic, and rather tiring to drive, but if it has any of the romance of motoring attached to it then you're happy. Old sports cars are a common Sagittarian purchase, because the sensation of actually travelling is usually stronger in them than in a quiet and well-insulated modern saloon.

Sagittarius has long been associated with horses. This may be the reason why some Sagittarians are attracted to cars which can be called 'thoroughbreds', in that they come from long-established names with a glorious past. MG, Riley, Alfa Romeo: these are Sagittarian cars, full of the romance of motoring, and far more attractive to you than the cold but efficient technology of today. You like their shapes — the curves of twenty years ago appeal more to Jupiter's sign than straight lines — and you like their colours, too: rich reds and maroons are more to Sagittarian taste than the silvers and greys which predominate today.

One car which associates itself with horses is the Range Rover, and it makes a perfect car for a Sagittarian, too. It is as tall as you are, giving you a higher and better view (*very* Sagittarian), and it can go anywhere, which is exactly what you want to do. The idea of being able to travel to the ends of the earth, over high mountains and across deserts, is one which constantly fascinates you, and cars which promise this, like Range Rovers and Jeeps, are something you would dearly love to own. As with the long-legged European touring car or the classic thoroughbred sports car, the practicalities of owning such things should really put you off buying one, but you always ignore little details like that. It is the ideal of travel, and the sensation of going places, which exert the strongest pull.

Food

Food to you is fuel, something that you need to keep up your active lifestyle. You enjoy it, and you like eating it, but it has to be said that you would probably enjoy it more if you ate it rather more slowly; Sagittarians wolf down their food.

There are some signs, notably Taurus, who make food into something close to a religion, and there are other signs, like Gemini, who hardly eat at all, and take little interest in what is set before them. You fall somewhere between the two.

Like the other two Fire signs, Aries and Leo, your appetite could be described as 'hearty'; you enjoy substantial meals whose main ingredient is meat. All the Fire signs like eating meat — Aries the most, it is said — but the Sagittarian speciality is game, both furred and feathered. It may be that the rich and strong flavours appeal to you, or it may be that the sign of the Archer feels that proper meat has to be hunted before it can be brought to the table; whichever it is, if the menu has pheasant or venison to offer, they'll be the ones you'll choose.

Nor is it hard to understand your liking for Indian and Chinese food. Anything which comes from far away, evoking that idea of distant places and long journeys, has a special appeal for you. So, too, does American food, the sort of food you can eat while you are on the move. Once again, it isn't the flavour, it's the idea of travel.

You are attracted by food which is rich or spicy in flavour, and which is a dark red in colour. Food which is pale, or whose predominant colour is green, seems less attractive to you. Red vegetables, like tomatoes, are fine — it's all to do with the colour.

Your favourite dish is probably something like goulash, which manages to combine most of the things that you like as far as colour, flavour and content goes. It also has the advantages of being foreign in origin, and being easy to eat, because it is an unfortunate fact that although Sagittarians have many talents, finesse at the table isn't one of them.

HOLIDAYS

You love going on holiday. You're addicted to the

process of travelling. Even the things that everybody else hates, such as waiting at the airport, or the flight itself, are fun for you. And since the travelling itself is so enjoyable, it doesn't really matter about the destination. Every destination is full of fascination for you, and the harder it is to get there, the better you like it.

It is quite possible that you would like to spend your entire holiday travelling; the idea of a plane ticket which enables you to cover the whole continental network served by a particular airline, or a round-the-world ticket, must appeal to you. So must the idea of a railpass, or of crossing Asia on the Trans-Siberian railway.

When you eventually get to where you're going, you don't head for the beach like everyone else, you explore the surrounding area. Sitting still isn't a rest for a Sagittarian, it's an illness; being active, mobile, inquisitive, finding things out, is what refreshes and restores you.

The places you would most like to visit are those which are part of the romantic traveller's tales of old: China, via the silk road, or India via the spice-trading routes. What you want is to feel that you have really travelled, and that the places you visit are very different from what you are used to. There's nothing worse, for you, than to go to some resort where every effort has been made to make things similar to the way they are at home.

For hundreds of years now, various countries of the world have been associated with the signs of the zodiac. Perhaps you might like to try visiting a few Sagittarian places. In Europe they include the whole of mainland Spain, the Tuscany region of Italy, and the Dalmatian coast of Yugoslavia. Further afield there's Arabia, and for those determined to go somewhere different, the island of Madagascar.

DRINKS

Sagittarius is a very social sign, and you usually enjoy visiting your local pub. Some signs go to pubs to drink, and some for company, but what Sagittarians do is get into long and involved philosophical discussions which last deep into the night. Philosophy and alcohol are both connected, astrologically, to Jupiter, so it's not surprising that Jupiter's sign has its best thoughts in the pub.

Like the other Fire signs, you stand or sit in plain view, unlike the Water signs, who hide in the corners, but you always make sure that you are in sight of the door. This isn't because you might need to escape, but so that you are the first to see if anyone new and interesting should walk in.

As always, you are attracted to things which come from far away. The local ale may be excellent, but if there is an imported beer from somewhere interesting like Czechoslovakia, then you'll have that, and spend the evening looking at the label on the bottle, imagining what the town must look like where it was brewed.

SPORTS AND PASTIMES

Sagittarians, along with Arians, are the great sportsmen of the zodiac. The difference between you is that Arians are individual performers, often choosing something like athletics, whereas Sagittarians are team members, preferring to play in company. You are also more likely to play games for their own sake; you like to win, of course, but you don't mind losing as long as you've had a good game. The English idea of sporting fair play is a very Sagittarian one.

The sign is supposed to have a liking for all equestrian sports. This is true, but it also has a liking for all motorized sports, and for all sports where the player gets muddy; cross-country running and rugby football are prime examples.

Riding and hunting are very close to the heart of the sign. All Sagittarian sports have a boisterous good humour to them, and are rather dirty, being connected to the countryside or to the farmyard in one sense or another. You have a natural scruffiness, an inability to stay clean, which doesn't matter at all when you're around dogs or horses, but which is part of the reasons why Sagittarians aren't usually attracted to tennis: the neatness and cleanness of the game and its costume are very un-Sagittarian.

Away from the playing field, Sagittarians play with travelling machines of all kinds, such as cars or old aeroplanes, and in the evenings you read. There is no subject which has no interest for you — you will read anything and everything, and to the disgust of the other eleven signs, you can remember most of it afterwards. Nothing is ever wasted on you: there is always something which is of value to you, and which you will be glad to know at some time in the future.

COLOUR AND STYLE

Sagittarians are not the zodiac's snappiest dressers. No matter how hard you try, you always look rather out of place in formal clothes, and you find them extremely uncomfortable; they make you feel stiff and unnatural, and you hate it.

What you need from your clothes is freedom of movement, and the ability to travel well. Formal clothes encourage you to stay still, and the pockets are usually too small to put anything useful in. Useful to a Sagittarian, that is, such as half a dozen books that you happen to be reading, or an interesting thing from a junkshop which you happened to buy on your way home.

You are at your best in soft, warm clothes, which suit your friendly and outdoor lifestyle. Most of the time you are happy in jeans and a sweater, and indeed some of you are quite likely to wear this combination to events and occasions with fairly strict dress codes, as if such things didn't apply to you. You reason that if you are going to be at your best, and enjoy yourself, then you have to be comfortable; if you feel strangled by your collar then you are unlikely to want to stay for long.

Every so often you decide that you need some more clothes, and go on a spending spree. What's unusual about this is that you have a tendency to buy rather flashy, expensive stuff (extravagance is one of Jupiter's qualities) which is probably unsuited to your lifestyle. It all becomes rather battered and well-worn in a few weeks anyway, because your rough-and-tumble life makes such demands on it.

Your favourite, and most useful, item of clothing is probably your jacket, and you are likely to have lots of them, probably in outdoor styles, such as waxed cotton shooting jackets, or down-filled ski jackets. The reason that you wear these rather than coats is that they don't hamper your legs, something which annoys you, and because they have lots of useful pockets.

You also like anything which is connected to the idea of travelling, such as flying jackets, or anything which suggests wide open spaces, such as Western styles. Motorcycle jackets are a favourite, too.

The preferred Sagittarian colour is always blue — preferably a deep shade, almost navy. You choose big motifs to match your big ideas, rather than fussy little prints, but most of the time you go for plain colours; they give a relaxed impression, and that's the most important thing about the Sagittarian style. It may not be chic, and it certainly isn't neat, but it's relaxed.

WORK

At work, you need to be involved in the transmission of ideas, and preferably to be mobile as well, if you are to feel at all satisfied. If your job has no opportunity for you to show what you can do and what you know, then it isn't for you. There is nothing which you cannot understand once you put your mind to it — Sagittarians are blessed with the finest mind in the zodiac — but there is a real risk that it will be under-used, and so you become bored.

What you must be particularly careful to avoid is anything which involves repetition, especially if the work itself is intricate or detailed, such as inspecting things for errors, or assembling small parts: in these circumstances your mind will refuse to operate properly, and you will make lots of mistakes. You need to be involved in bigger things, basically.

Lots of Sagittarians are teachers, which suits your abilities very well. It's a lively, talkative sort of job, but it's also one where you get a chance to give other people the benefit of your knowledge, which is something that gives you great satisfaction of the kind which is so deep that you can't easily describe it to someone who doesn't know the feeling for themselves. The same applies to medicine, which is another Sagittarian profession: it's to do with applying your knowledge for the benefit of others.

Knowledge is something you Sagittarians value highly, and a career either publishing or selling books will appeal. So will anything connected with languages, such as translating, or perhaps dealing with books and magazines in foreign languages.

Two old and respectable professions which have always been connected to the sign are the legal profession in all its various forms, and the Church. As always with Sagittarius, the business of both of these lies with ideas rather than objects.

Some Sagittarians prefer their work to be out of doors and to keep them mobile. The transportation and haulage trades are full of Sagittarians at all levels who prefer to be on the move than to be behind a desk all day, even if their career development becomes limited. Freedom always outweighs money to this sign.

Finally, animals, and specifically horses, always have a place in your affections. Sagittarians can be found racing, breeding and riding horses; as vets; and as bookies, tipsters, and gamblers, too. Wherever there are horses, there are Sagittarians.

To sum up, things to go for:
- Any job which gives you a chance to use what you know;
- Any job which is changeable and has no set routine;
- Any job which involves travel.

Things to avoid:
- Fine detail work;
- Jobs where strict rules are kept to and independence is frowned on;
- Jobs where the end product is an object rather than an idea.

PEOPLE

You like people who are:
- outgoing;
- optimistic;
- open and forthright.

You dislike people who:
- take life too seriously;
- have no belief in providence;
- deliberately mislead or take advantage of others.

Love-Hate Chart

Who are the People you
don't get on with?

Most astrology books have a section in them where they say which signs are compatible with yours. That's all very well, but the thing you could really use, most of the time, is some sort of indication as to which signs you *don't* get on with, so that you know what you're in for when you are introduced to somebody for the first time. This is especially useful when you find yourself sitting opposite somebody new in the office; you're going to spend nearly half your waking day with them, five days a week, and although knowing whether you are 'compatible' is all very well if you are trying to marry them, it's not a great deal of use if you're trying to make some sort of a working relationship.

Here, then, is something a little different — a table of the signs which tells you how well, or how badly, they get on with each other. The higher the score, the more arguments the pair of you are likely to have; the lower the score, the easier it will be for the pair of you to get along — though both of you may sometimes need a kick in the rear to get you moving.

You are likely to be most interested in the scores which apply to your own sign, of course, but the others are all included so that you can have some fun working out what your friends are having to deal with in their own relationships. Not only is this great fun, but it enables you to be as nosy as you like without anyone knowing!

THEM YOU	Aries	Taurus	Gemini	Cancer	Leo	Virgo	Libra	Scorpio	Sagittarius	Capricorn	Aquarius	Pisces
Aries	6	9	2	7	3	7	4	6	3	5	2	8
Taurus	9	6	8	2	6	4	6	4	7	3	6	1
Gemini	2	8	5	8	2	4	3	7	4	7	3	8
Cancer	6	1	8	5	8	2	6	6	7	4	7	3
Leo	2	6	2	7	5	7	3	4	3	7	4	7
Virgo	7	3	5	2	8	4	8	2	7	3	7	5
Libra	4	6	3	6	2	9	5	9	2	6	3	6
Scorpio	6	4	7	4	6	2	9	6	8	1	6	3
Sagittarius	3	7	4	6	3	7	2	8	5	9	2	5
Capricorn	7	3	7	4	8	3	5	2	8	6	5	3
Aquarius	3	6	3	8	4	7	2	6	2	7	5	8
Pisces	8	2	7	2	7	4	7	3	5	3	8	5

Love-Hate Chart

Of course, this chart works for *all* relationships, not just romances, and not just for male-female, either. So, you can use it to find out why you keep arguing with your father, your sister, even your boss; it tells you the truth about all of them.

How to use the chart
It couldn't be easier. Find your own sign going down the left hand column, then read across to find how you score with another person from each of the twelve signs.

Make sure you remember which one is you and

which one is the other person, because the answer isn't the same in both directions. For example, a Leo gets a score of 2 with an Aries, but the Aries gets a score of 3 with a Leo. This means that the Leo finds the Aries slightly easier to get on with than the Aries finds the Leo, and so if there are any arguments it will usually be the Aries who starts them, and the Aries who loses his temper first.

INTERPRETING THE SCORES

Score 1   *Too Easy*.
This is the relationship with almost no friction at all in it. The two of you understand each other's point of view perfectly, and you know instinctively what to do to please each other. At times, you are almost the same person, because it is very easy for you to make the slight changes to your opinions and tastes which will bring you into perfect alignment. The trouble with this arrangement is that relationships actually work better if there's a little bit of friction, so that each partner can bring out the best of the other, and so that each of you can do things that you wouldn't have tried if you had been on your own. With this relationship it isn't like that, though, because you are so close; what happens instead is that you let yourselves get lazy, and you both slip back into your old bad habits, doing the sort of things that you know you shouldn't.

Score 2   *Very Easy*.
This is the 'best-of-friends' relationship, where the two of you get on very well and really enjoy each other's company. It's usually a very talkative relationship, where the two of you find that you have endless things to talk about, and love nothing better than to sit with each other over a drink, and to lay out all your dreams and plans for the future. It doesn't matter that

none of these plans ever seem to be put into action, or that you change them from day to day; you just enjoy being with each other, and you *like* each other. It's as simple as that. You don't have arguments very often, firstly because you like each other too much, and secondly because this is a light and mobile relationship, and disagreement seems too heavy a thing to bring into it. If there are areas where you don't meet eye-to-eye, then you simply pass them by and talk about something else. There's always something new to talk about, so why cause unpleasantness?

Score 3   *Easy*
This is the relationship where each partner finds qualities in the other which he really admires, and wishes he had in himself. When you are with this person, you are constantly hoping that by being with them, some of their style, sense of humour, confidence, or whatever, will rub off on you. Whenever they do something, you find yourself thinking, 'That's really good, I wish I'd thought of that'. It's not all one-way traffic, though; in fact, the two of you show off and reflect each other's talents very well, so it brings out the best in both of you. The only time that you argue is when one of you thinks that the other is doing something in a way that you *wouldn't* like to copy. You will find yourself saying, 'I wish you wouldn't do that!' Think about why you say that: what you wish is that they'd do it in a way that you would like to do it yourself. Luckily, it doesn't happen often; most of the time this pairing reminds you of all the things you like best about yourself and can see in the other person.

Score 4   *Variable*
This is where the major differences start to creep in. With this score, there are going to be an increasing number of occasions when the two of you seem to hold exactly opposite views on how best to do something.

It's quite funny to watch, for an outsider, because your views aren't actually very different — just opposite. In practice, it means that the relationship goes up and down a bit; sometimes you both do things your way, and sometimes your partner's way. What you have going for you is that you share the same basic outlook on life, and the things that are really important to you are important to both of you. You don't have to go round trying to explain the way you feel to somebody who seems to have no comprehension of what you're on about. There is a tendency for the pair of you to have similar weaknesses, which makes it difficult for one to help the other, but that's true to some extent for all the low-score relationships.

Score 5 *Brisk, workable.*
This is the half-way score, balanced between perfect alignment and constant conflict. There are likely to be a fair number of arguments with this relationship, but they won't last long, and they are usually productive, in that they release frustrations, help communication, and stimulate growth. Most of the combinations which produce a score of 5 are from two people of the same sign, and those that aren't are from signs which have other factors in common. This means that there is a great deal of *understanding* with this score; you may not like what the other person does all of the time, but you can understand why he feels the way he does, because you would feel that way yourself if you were in his or her shoes. You never get the feeling that this person is something very alien to you, somebody whose soul you can never hope to understand. This familiarity means that you can accept your differences with a grin and a shrug of the shoulders. You forgive each other, but you know that there will be more arguments sometime in the future. You don't mind: you'd still rather have this person as a friend than some others you could think of.

Score 6   *Challenging.*
With this relationship the differences start to become
more obvious than the similarities, and you realize quite
early on that you are two different people who need to
develop a system of give and take if you are to get
along together. In fact, things could be much worse,
and you are usually able to recognize in each other the
strengths and talents that you yourself don't have. You
will also notice that you are both successful in your own
areas, each in ways that the other just couldn't manage.
Following on from this comes a sort of admiration for
each other's differences, and you start to defend each
other when necessary, as in 'He may not be very
ambitious, but he's very kind and considerate, and I like
that'. If you don't learn to appreciate each other's
strengths, you simply criticize each other for being
different, and the relationship never gets a chance to
grow. If you both give your talents to the relationship,
and don't interfere in each other's areas unless asked,
this can be a very strong and successful union.

Score 7   *Adjustment needed.*
This score usually indicates a relationship where the
two people are so different that they are unlikely to
have any points of contact. That's not necessarily a bad
thing, because at least you leave each other alone to
get on with what you have to do, but it does mean that
you have to make positive and determined efforts to
form a relationship; you can't just muddle along and
hope that something will grow, because it probably
won't. You are essentially separate people, with
separate aims and interests, and that makes it very
difficult for you even to understand, let alone appreciate or share, what the other person is trying to do. You
will have to try to understand how they see things, try to
put yourself in their position, and try to see what they
are aiming for. It's not easy, for either of you, but if you
can bridge the gap in any way you will be able to help

each other out and solve each other's problems in ways that you wouldn't have imagined possible. It's a real long-term commitment, this one, and it's not for the selfish or the lazy.

Score 8   *Difficult.*
The appealing thing about a relationship like this, especially at the beginning, is the very high level of involvement. You just don't seem to be able to ignore each other, and that's an encouraging start. You just don't seem to be able to agree on anything, either, but you keep trying, because you both believe that you're right, and that with just a little more persuasion the other person will be able to see your point of view and come over to your side. In fact, it seldom gets any better, and you could easily stay like that, arguing back and forth forever. Much of the problem comes from an absolute refusal to do things any way but your own, and you feel that to even try things their way just once would be letting them win, and you won't have that. It's a pity that this relationship boils down to being a simple contest in so many cases; what it highlights is the lack of confidence each person has in himself. If you can stop fighting for a moment, and believe that you won't somehow die by doing things *their* way, you will be able to see how much they have to offer you that you need and can't do for yourself.

Score 9   *Extremely difficult.*
This score is thankfully rare, and is only possible with certain combinations of signs which are next to each other. What makes 9 different from an 8 is that the other person's viewpoint and way of working specifically blocks your own, so that not only are your actions in conflict with his, but his actions prevent you from functioning properly by taking away the very things you need most. The result is that you feel completely unable to be yourself, and that makes you depressed. Either

you let yourself be completely controlled and ordered by them, which is a bad thing, or you have massive confrontations every so often where you demand the freedom, or the space, or whatever it is, to be yourself and to feel happy and contented. After a while they will close in on you again, and you will have to fight for your space once more; the process will go on and on. To make this one work you must learn to live in the same space without treading on each other. If you can do that, the relationship can be quiet, safe and long-lasting; if you can't, you'll destroy each other.

Faces and Bodies

Being a Sagittarius involves more than just ways of thinking and feeling — it influences the way you look, too. The twelve zodiac signs each have a set of physical features associated with them, and your birthday will determine which set you get to wear. The reason that there aren't many small and compact Sagittarians is that being small and compact comes with Capricorn and not with Sagittarius, and the only people you can blame for being in the wrong sign are your parents!

Over the last couple of thousand years, astrologers have spent a lot of time matching faces to birthdays and to times of birth, and have produced descriptions which are not just linked to the month of your birth, but to the day or the hour as well. Once you know your way round them, you will be able to see not only how closely *you* fit the pattern, but spot other Sagittarians as well.

Here's the basic Sagittarian; see how many of the key features match your own.

General outline:
Long. Sagittarius gives the longest limbs in the whole zodiac, especially the legs, but it isn't as thin and narrow-looking as the Virgo or the Gemini physique, so although the length of the frame is noticeable, it doesn't look short of muscle. It's an athletic frame, but not as densely muscled or as powerful across the shoulders as the Arian or Taurean. The head is long like the rest of

the body, and is carried high; this, too, makes the shoulders seem less broad. Sometimes there is a stoop, caused by years of talking to people of shorter stature and ducking through low doorways.

Height:
Medium to tall, sometimes very tall.

Hair:
Traditionally, light to mid brown. It should be strong in growth and glossy. There is a tendency for a high hairline, often unkindly referred to as 'receding'.

Complexion:
Healthy-looking, with a good colour, not often pale. Sometimes rather flushed, with strong colour in the cheeks.

Distinguishing features:
The mobility of the body is noticeable. There is a looseness to the movements which suggests that the Sagittarian is not paying much attention to his posture or to where he is putting his hands and his feet. Some signs look very tightly-knit and rather rigid, but not this one. Sagittarians are constantly on the move, unable to stay still for long; they walk well, but sit awkwardly.

Face:
Like the body, the face is quite long. The Sagittarian face has often been compared to that of a horse, and there is some truth in it. The nose is prominent, firm and straight, and the eyes are wide but kindly, taking a friendly interest in everything that happens. The mouth is full and broad, but the length of the face prevents it from appearing either too fleshy or in any way lascivious.

Rising Signs

It's quite easy to make a sort of 'Identikit' portrait of a Sagittarian from that. The basic description can be modified a little according to whether you were born early or late in the sign. Sagittarians born at the beginning or the end of the sign are supposedly the tallest, while the most solidly built come from the early part of December. Those born in the middle of December have the most attractive features, it is said.

This is all very well, but you probably have a couple of Sagittarian friends who look quite different from you, even if you do have a few things in common like grey eyes or long legs. This is because the thing which has the biggest influence on the way you look is your *rising sign*. The rising sign is the one which was rising on the eastern horizon when you were born. During the 24 hours of your birthday all twelve signs will have risen at some time or other, giving twelve different sorts of Sagittarian. You will still be a Sagittarian, of course, because of the date, but even if someone shares your birthday they will look very different from you if the times of day at which the two of you were born are different by more than an hour or two. You could be a Aries-type Sagittarian, for example, and they could be a Libra-type Sagittarian.

Working out the rising sign — or Ascendant, to give it its proper name — is a bit lengthy, so there is a graph over the page to help. You simply look up your time of birth along the top, your birthday down the side, and see where they cross. Don't forget to subtract an hour for Summer Time, or anything like that. If you were born at 2.15 a.m. on 10th December, for example, your rising sign is Libra.

To make the graph easy to use, the values it gives have been fixed to be correct for the South of England. As you go north from there, by more than a couple of hundred miles, the values change; the narrow stripes

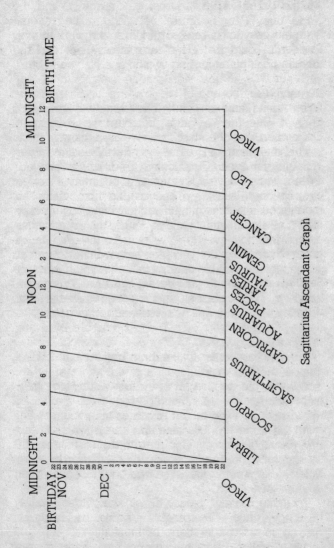

Sagittarius Ascendant Graph

on the graph (Aries, Taurus) get narrower, and the wide ones (Virgo, Libra) get wider. The reverse happens as you go south. If it looks as though in your case you could be one of two signs, then read the descriptions given and see which one fits you best.

Aries rising

With Aries rising you get height, even if the Sun sign is a 'short' one. You also get a characteristic 'fiery' look in the eyes, a sort of flash or sparkle which shows a lively and challenging spirit. The eyebrows become larger, too, and the eyes themselves more deep-set. The face is less broad at the bottom, and becomes a sort of triangle, wide at the top, and with a pointed chin.

With this rising sign there is almost no body fat at all. The frame is athletic, fit and flat rather than curvaceous.

The real giveaway to Aries rising is the tremendous sense of energy. There is always movement; you tend to lean forward all the time, as though running, because you are so eager to get started. With Aries rising you speak in short sentences, and you don't waste time with idle gossip — you are decisive, and to the point.

Taurus rising

Taurus rising gives all the broad, solid build which makes the Sun sign famous, and will add weight and solidity to the upper part of the body. The face gains soft features — soft enough even to give dimpled cheeks — and the mouth becomes fuller but smaller, with the upper lip the same size as the lower, to give the cherub's mouth of Cupid. With this sort of face the eyes are blue or brown, not often green or grey. Hair is thick and naturally wavy. The face is rather square, with a wide jaw.

The Taurus rising person moves slowly, deliberately, and never rushes things. When sitting, he is relaxed, not nervous or on the edge of the seat.

The really noticeable thing about Taurus rising

people is the feeling that they are generously built, made to a quality and not to a price. No part of them is thin, pinched, or sparse, and their deep, melodious voices reflect the very real pleasure they get from living in such a frame.

Gemini rising

To have this sign rising is usually to be thinner and more slightly built than the Sun sign might suggest. The predominant direction is the vertical — in no places is this person particularly wide, though some very ancient authorities thought that this sign gave weight to the hips and thighs. The face is usually long, with long features, especially the nose. The forehead is very pronounced, and is both high and round, with the temples noticeable. Eyes are small but very alert, and have a glint as they notice things. The whole face is very mobile and rather sharp-looking, with many changes of expression.

Gemini rising people wave their hands and arms about a great deal, and they walk quickly but with a light step. They are always, it seems, on the move, never relaxed or static. They talk a lot, too, and they ask questions; they have a general air of being inquisitive, and they like to know what's going on.

Cancer rising

The noticeable thing about the appearance of anyone with Cancer rising is how *round* they are, like the Full Moon. The face is almost a circle to look at, with the features set in the middle of what seems like a great expanse and looking rather small. There don't seem to be any firm lines in the face; the jawline is indistinct, and the chiselled cheekbones that characterize other signs just aren't there. Complexion is often rather pale, and the colour of the eyes too; it's as though all the colouring were somehow diluted, made weaker, by having Cancer rising. The hair, too, is usually fairer in colour than, say, parents or family might lead you to expect.

With Cancer rising the body is bigger than the limbs, and can be a bit flabby. The arms and legs tend to be short and a bit thin. It's not a muscular sign, so the firmness of signs like Aries isn't there. These people put on extra weight easily, especially the men, though they're not heavy in their movements.

Leo rising

Leo rising produces an unmistakable physique. The face is broad and handsome, but not fat, because the bone structure is usually visible. The whole head seems to have been built on a generous scale, and no feature is small or narrow. The forehead in particular is both broad and high, and the eyes look out with confidence and clarity from beneath heroic brows. The head is always carried high and level. Leo rising people face their world unruffled and unafraid; they don't look away shyly, screw up their eyes, look at the ground, stand with their heads bowed, or anything like that at all. There is a sort of golden glow to the face, often from the colour of the complexion or the hair, though not entirely. The hair is often golden yellow, and the desire for it to be so is strong enough to tempt those with darker hair to colour it until the golden mane is achieved. And that word 'mane' is just right, because the hair seems to stand off the head for about an inch or so before sweeping back. Leo hair is never limp or straight; it has *body*, and again those few whose hair lacks this quality will style and treat it so that it appears to have it.

All Leo rising people are as tall as they can be. They walk with their head up, their shoulders back, and their spine straight; they never ever stoop or slouch. The overall impression of someone with Leo rising is of confidence and superiority, all overlaid with that recognizable 'goldenness'.

Virgo rising

Your ears are likely to tell you that someone has Virgo rising before your eyes do. With Virgo rising, the voice becomes very penetrating. It is traditionally supposed to be thin or shrill, but other factors in the horoscope may modify this. Whatever its tone, though, it seems to cut through whatever else is going on — music, conversation — and be the voice you can't help but hear.

Facially, Virgo rising gives a narrow face, rather pointed at times, and certainly with pointed features quite common, such as the nose or chin. No part of the face is heavy, and neither is any feature particularly large.

There is a sort of light-brownishness to Virgo rising, which affects hair and eye colour: extremes of fair and dark colouring aren't usually found with this sign rising.

The physique is narrow, even willowy, with a very long waist in many cases; breadth and bulk, either from muscle or from fat, don't seem to go with this sign. There is a noticeable neatness, even fussiness, about Virgo rising, which is quite easy to spot because these people are forever fidgeting, putting things straight and picking at this and that.

Libra rising

With Libra rising the most obvious thing is how easy on the eye everything is. The face and the figure are both balanced and even, with nothing too big, too small, out of balance or out of proportion. The forehead is high, but not too broad, and is balanced by the lower half of the face, which matches its shape, so that an even effect is achieved. Though the face is rounded (no pointed features or heavy bones), it isn't circular, and so the overall impression is an attractive oval.

Some Libra rising people have 'angelic' features, in that they have large round eyes, small but full lips, and a small nose. The general tendency with the Libran face is for everything to be round and soft anyway; one thing that this face isn't — in any way — is rugged.

The influence of the planet Venus gives a certain elegance, a grace of movement to the body. It's quite difficult to find someone with Libra rising who is heavy-footed or clumsy, though their elegance isn't the sort of thing you notice until you look for it.

Scorpio rising

Here the physique is rather small, even if the Sun sign position suggests the opposite. Small doesn't mean light, though; the body can be quite broad, and in any case it seems to be quite heavy for its size. Some of the weight is muscle, because Scorpio rising produces quite a powerful body, but some of it is fat, and this sign puts on weight quite easily. The shoulder and neck area is often well-developed, but a narrow waist is uncommon, so the body outline is more of a cone than an hourglass.

Facially, the most obvious thing about Scorpio rising is the intensity of the gaze. To be eye to eye with someone with Scorpio rising is sometimes a disconcerting experience. The eyes are usually very dark in colour, and set wide and deep beneath a very strong brow and forehead. The overall impression of the face is that it is immensely strong and rather dangerous. The jawline is well-defined, especially in men, but the features are often soft and full. Colouring tends towards the darker end of the available range, and a pale complexion is very rare.

Sagittarius rising

To have Sagittarius rising *and* the Sun in Sagittarius makes you a double Sagittarius. You should therefore look like the description of the basic Sagittarius — only more so.

Capricorn rising

Capricorn rising makes the body leaner and bonier, and probably shorter, too, whatever the Sun sign. The shoulders seem to stick out, and the head is worn slightly forwards, between them, bowed forwards a little. It's quite difficult to get these people to stand up straight, and they lean forwards again when they walk.

Facially, Capricorn rising gives a very visible bone structure, which can be very attractive, though looking a little cold. The jaw is strongly developed, and may be rather heavy, with lines in the face to emphasize it. Many of the facial features, particularly the corners of the mouth and eyes, point downwards, and remain that way even in laughter, which is quite easy to spot. The skin is pale, and is likely to be in the cream to yellow range of complexion colours rather than the pinks or golden tones.

Movements and gestures are stiff and restricted, as much as is necessary and no more. The overall impression of the person is of someone who takes life rather seriously, and doesn't expect to enjoy it much.

Aquarius rising

The most distinctive characteristic in the appearance given by this sign rising is how clean-cut and clear all the features become. The features and physique given by the Sun sign aren't altered much at all, but somehow all the ill-defined or slightly sloppy elements get removed, and the result is a much cleaner and lighter look altogether. Aquarius rising emphasizes the vertical rather the horizontal dimension, but it doesn't make anyone too tall or too thin — just slimmer.

The face is usually a narrow oval, and the complexion is noticeably clear. The features are neat and regular, never large enough to dominate the face. There is traditionally a hint of reddish-brown somewhere in the sign, giving sandy hair or hazel eyes from time to time.

If you watch these people, you will notice that they

seldom touch anything with any part of themselves unless they intend to. Some people blunder down the street bumping into almost everything, but Aquarius rising people seem to be able to keep themselves apart from all that; they have a distinct *separateness*.

Pisces rising

Pisces rising gives the least firm outline of all the signs. Often the weight is concentrated in the lower half of the body, or even of the individual limbs, and the shoulders are quite rounded. Weight gain is easy for this sign, and it often seems to go on in all the wrong places. The strong framework of the body and the musculature which holds it in shape, seem to be entirely absent in this case. Movement, which relies on muscles, is frequently rather clumsy.

The predominant facial feature tends to be the eyes, which can be heavy-lidded and rather sleepy looking, but not unattractive. The complexion is pale, as is the eye colour too — traditionally pale blue or green. The mouth is often very soft and full, and since the face is often large and soft anyway, double chins come quite easily.

The whole person seems not to have been designed for strength or sustained effort, and it's the general lack of robustness which is perhaps the most noticeable thing.

THE TRUTH ABOUT BEING BORN *ON THE CUSP*

Life can sometimes be confusing if your birthday is at the end of the third week of the month. In one magazine it will say that Sagittarius starts on 22nd November, but in another it will say that Sagittarius starts on the 23rd, and that anyone who was born on the 22nd is a late Scorpio.

'But I don't feel like a Scorpio!' you cry, 'I feel like a Sagittarian!' The answer you usually get is that you were born *on the cusp*, a mysterious area where the Sun is neither one sign nor the other, and where the qualities of both signs can be found mingled together.

It's a good word, *cusp*. It's the sort of word you'd never find outside astrology, so you go away with ideas of it meaning some sort of grey area where two things are possible at once, a place where you can be either, or both, of two zodiacal characters. It's nothing of the sort, actually. The word cusp means a *point*, a *tip*; the Sun changes from Scorpio into Sagittarius at a single point in time, and there is never a time when it is in both at once. There is no vague area where they join — you're either one or the other, and that's that.

So why do magazines tell you all this stuff about cusps? Why do they move the dates around? Does Sagittarius start on the 22nd, or the 23rd?

Well, actually, it's a white lie, to save having to go into a long explanation, and because it used to be thought that nobody really wanted to know. But it seems that everybody with a birthday anywhere near the change of signs really does want to know which one they really are — so here is the real answer.

It's all to do with the calendar. On a calendar the year is 365 days long, but the Sun isn't so neat in making its annual trip round the zodiac; it takes 365 days, 5 hours, 48 minutes, and 46 seconds. The calendar catches up the difference by having an extra day every four years, making a leap year, and it makes further fine tuning by *not* having leap years at the ends of the centuries unless the number is divisible by 400. It still isn't quite right, but it's quite good, and it will be a few thousand years yet before the difference is enough for us to worry about.

The trouble comes when you try and fix a position from one system to the other. The first moment of Sagittarius may be on the 22nd one year, but it may be on the 23rd the next. Those spare five hours and all the minutes and seconds may take you forward into the early hours of the next day. Then there's the leap year to consider, and a few other things besides. It's a tricky business.

Your birthday is fixed, of course. You know the date, the year, the time. What isn't so certain is that the Sun was in Sagittarius at that moment: you will need to find out on what date, and at what time, that the Sun entered Sagittarius, or left it, in that year.

Magazine astrologers have two choices; either they could take an average date, like the 22nd, and accept that for some years they will be wrong, or they could print a whole list of years and times so that the readers could sort out for themselves which sign they really were. Such a list (times twelve, of course, for all the signs) would take up a great deal of space, so that's why they don't do it. They go for the average date option, instead. Sometimes they pick the 22nd, and sometimes the 23rd, but it really doesn't matter; the dates are only there as a guide.

But here, for people who really want to know, is the other option — a table of the dates and the times when the Sun went into Sagittarius, and when it went out into Capricorn, so now you check which one you really are, and which horoscopes you should be reading in your favourite magázine. It may mean, of course, that you discover that you are not a Sagittarius after all, you will have to buy another *Sun Sign Secrets* book for your new sign!

The times in this table are in GMT, so that if you were born outside the UK, you can adjust for the time zone difference. Don't forget that from 1940-44 there was *permanent* Summer Time, and from 1968-71, too.

Year	**Into Sagittarius** Date (November)	time	**Out of Sagittarius** Date (December)	time
1940[1]	22nd	10.49	21st	23.55
1941[1]	22nd	16.48	22nd	05.44
1942[1]	22nd	22.30	22nd	11.40
1943[1]	23rd	04.21	22nd	17.29
1944[1]	22nd	10.08	21st	23.15
1945	22nd	15.55	22nd	05.04
1946	22nd	21.46	22nd	10.53
1947	23rd	03.38	22nd	16.43
1948	22nd	09.29	21st	22.33
1949	22nd	15.16	22nd	04.23
1950	22nd	21.03	22nd	10.13
1951	23rd	02.51	22nd	16.00
1952	22nd	08.36	21st	21.43
1953	22nd	14.22	22nd	03.31
1954	22nd	20.14	22nd	09.24
1955	23rd	02.01	22nd	15.11
1956	22nd	07.50	21st	21.00
1957	22nd	13.39	22nd	02.49
1958	22nd	19.29	22nd	08.40
1959	23rd	01.27	22nd	14.34
1960	22nd	07.18	21st	20.26
1961	22nd	13.08	22nd	02.20
1962	22nd	19.02	22nd	08.15
1963	23rd	00.49	22nd	14.02
1964	22nd	06.39	21st	19.50
1965	22nd	12.29	22nd	01.41
1966	22nd	18.14	22nd	07.28
1967	23rd	00.05	22nd	13.16
1968[1]	22nd	05.49	21st	19.00
1969[1]	22nd	11.31	22nd	00.44
1970[1]	22nd	17.25	22nd	06.36
1971[1]	22nd	23.14	22nd	12.24

1972	22nd	05.03	21st	18.13
1973	22nd	10.54	22nd	00.08
1974	22nd	16.39	22nd	05.56
1975	22nd	22.31	22nd	11.46
1976	22nd	04.22	21st	17.35
1977	22nd	10.07	21st	23.23
1978	22nd	16.05	22nd	05.21
1979	22nd	21.54	22nd	11.10
1980	22nd	03.42	21st	16.56
1981	22nd	09.36	21st	22.51
1982	22nd	15.24	22nd	04.39
1983	22nd	21.19	22nd	10.30
1984	22nd	03.11	21st	16.23
1985	22nd	08.51	21st	22.08
1986	22nd	14.45	22nd	04.03
1987	22nd	20.30	22nd	09.46
1988	22nd	02.12	21st	15.28
1989	22nd	08.05	21st	21.22
1990	22nd	13.47	22nd	03.07
1991	22nd	19.36	22nd	08.54
1992	22nd	01.26	21st	14.44
1993	22nd	07.07	21st	20.26
1994	22nd	13.06	22nd	02.23
1995	22nd	19.02	22nd	08.17

[1]Time one hour ahead of GMT all year round in the UK in these years.

THE OTHER SAGITTARIANS

WHO SHARES YOUR BIRTHDAY?

It's fun to see who else shares your birthday. Anybody
who shares your birthday, or is within a day of it (for the
reason why you can be a day each side, see The Truth
About Being Born *On The Cusp* on p. 49) will represent
the same degree of the zodiac as you do, and that
means that although you won't necessarily look like
them, you will be similar in character. Just think —
nobody will know what somebody famous is *really* like,
but *you* will, because you share a birthday with them.
They're just like you, in lots of way.

There's a zesty, vivid quality about Sagittarians. Larger
and frequently louder, than most people, they have a
unique combination of energy and optimism which
enables them to get away with things that the other
eleven signs can only dream of.

This swashbuckling quality found itself perfectly
expressed in Hollywood by Douglas Fairbanks Jr,
whose birthday is 9th December. He shares his
birthday with another heroic leading man from the
movies, Kirk Douglas. Other Sagittarians from the great
day of the movies include Boris Karloff, the original
Frankenstein's monster, born right at the beginning of
the sign on 23rd November, and Edward G. Robinson,
who was born on 12th December. His birthday is also
that of Frank Sinatra, whose tremendous talent com-
bines with a strong sense of independence in a way

which is entirely typical of the sign. Jane Fonda, whose birthday is 21st December, has these qualities, too.

A similar confidence in his own abilities can be seen in Ian Botham, born on 24th November, while the Sagittarian's ability to bounce back from misfortune is well demonstrated by Tina Turner, who is two days later, on the 26th. Rolling Stone Keith Richards is a Sagittarian, too — 18th December is his birthday.

Sometimes Sagittarian behaviour goes beyond what some people think reasonable. Jonathan King and Bette Midler are both from the sign: her birthday is the 1st, and his the 6th.

The sharp way with words which they both have is a particular Sagittarian ability, and there are many who have become famous for it. Billy Connolly is another good example, sharing Ian Botham's birthday on the 24th, but there's also Noel Coward, whose birthday was the 16th, and the remarkable 'double' of Mark Twain, the first author to use a typewriter (a forward-thinking Sagittarian), and Jonathan Swift, the satirist author of *Gulliver's Travels*. Twain and Swift were both born on 30th November.

30th November was also Churchill's birthday. He is just one of a number of important world figures who had a major part to play in the Second World War. General de Gaulle was a Sagittarian from 22nd November, right at the start of the sign. The Spanish dictator General Franco was born on 4th December, while the King of England at the time, George VI, had his birthday on the 14th — and his younger brother the Duke of Kent was a Sagittarian too, on the 20th.

Vision and imagination, coupled with a sense of wonderment, are an essential part of every Sagittarian. Two Sagittarians whose imagination has delighted millions are Walt Disney, whose birthday was 5th December, and Steven Spielberg, who celebrates on the 18th. Earlier imaginative Sagittarians had to rely on painting and poetry to communicate their ideas:

William Blake's birthday was 30th November, while Christina Rosetti's was 5th December. A different sort of imagination is shown by Charles Schulz (26th November), creator of the *Peanuts* cartoons; their penetrating yet kindly insight into the way we all feel is very Sagittarian.

Finally, two Sagittarians whose vision extends even into the far future: the seer Nostradamus, born on 14th December, and Arthur C. Clarke, whose birthday is two days later on the 16th.

ALL THE SAME BUT DIFFERENT

One of the questions that astrologers usually get asked is that if everybody is different and unique and individual, how can all the people in the world from one Sun sign be the same?

The answer is that everyone from each of the twelve Sun signs has just one thing in common – their Sun sign. They each have many other things about them, however, which are *not* shared by everyone else, and that's what makes them all different.

When an astrologer draws a chart for a single individual, he looks at the position in the sky not just of the Sun, but of all the other planets as well, from Mercury out to Pluto. Just because the Sun may be in Libra doesn't mean that the other planets will be: as I write this, in late 1988, Jupiter is in Gemini and Saturn is in Sagittarius, for example. This means that someone born in October might well think of themselves as a Libran, because of the Sun's position, but there are also going to be parts of them which are like a Gemini or a Sagittarian, or whatever.

This happens because the planets don't go round the zodiac at the same speed as the Sun. Some of them stay for months, or even years, in the same sign, while at the other extreme the Moon goes round the whole twelve signs in just under a month, changing signs every two and a half days.

It would be just as true to say that all the people born

when Venus was in Capricorn have something in common with each other as it is to say that all the people born with the Sun in Taurus have, but it's very unlikely that you'll ever see horoscopes in magazines for such people to read, and for two good reasons.

Firstly, the Sun's motions are linked to the calendar: each year on a given date the Sun is more or less in the same part of the zodiac, so as long as you know your birthday, you know which sign the Sun is in. Venus's motion doesn't match the calendar at all, and so the magazines and newspapers would have to print large lists to say that Venus was in this sign on this date in this year, and so on, which is all very inconvenient.

Secondly, the Sun is the strongest influence, astrologically. To show what you are according to your Sun sign describes the main part of your personality, whereas to describe what you are according to your Venus sign of Mars sign only shows a little bit. An important bit, sure, but not as central as the Sun sign description.

Only when *all* the planets' influences are taken into account does the full picture emerge. It is this, the combination of all the planets in all their various signs, and the parts of the sky they occupy at the moment of your birth, and at the place of your birth, which makes up a horoscope, and each one is different. The number of combinations is far from twelve, or even twelve times twelve; the answer is in billions of billions, more than enough for every person who ever lived to have a different horoscope, and to last us for a million years to come.

Mind-boggling thought, isn't it? They are all different, and yet because so many of them share common elements, such as the Sun in a particular sign, they are to some extent the same.

Something that isn't done very often, but which is quite an eye-opener, is to have a look at the groups of people who have the slow-moving planets in the same sign. Take Uranus as an example: it takes seven years for it to pass through just one sign of the zodiac, and so every single person born during that time, no matter where no no matter what their Sun sign, will have Uranus's influence in the same sign, and so have something in common with everyone else born during that time.

You may be wondering what it is that you have in common with everybody else born within a few years of you, since you all look different and do different things, but what links you all together is something bigger than that. What we're labelling here is *generations*. Here are the children of the Depression, the Baby Boomers, the Rock 'n' Rollers, the Hippies – generations with their own particular styles and beliefs. This is why tastes change every few years. What happens is that a new group of people come to maturity who were born at a time when the outer planets were in another sign.

On the next page there is a graph which shows you how the big planets moved through the zodiac in the middle years of this century. Have a look to see where they were when you were born. Have a look for somebody who is a few years younger than you, and who appears to represent a different generation. You will see that the planets have changed signs. Now have a look for the year when an older relative, perhaps your mother or father, was born. The difference between your planetary placings and theirs is the zodiacal version of the generation gap, and it shows why your tastes in, say, music, are so different from those of an older person, even if your Sun signs are the same. These outer planet positions are the things which really 'date' us, no matter how hard we try to keep up!

Here's a quick guide to what was when, for use with the graph.

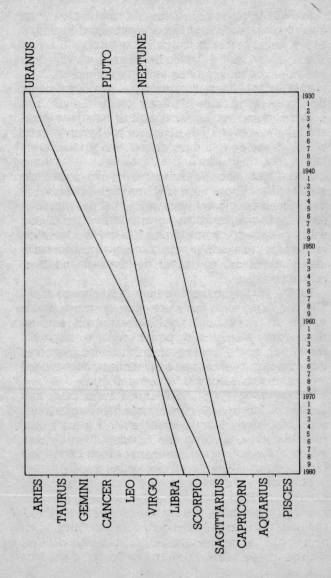

Pre – 1938: Neptune in Virgo and Pluto in Cancer for everybody gives a strong feeling for family and country, and a belief in doing things in the proper manner. These are the children of the Depression, who become the 'older generation' to the teenagers of the '60s.

1938 – 1941: Pluto changes signs, into Leo. People born now place more emphasis on themselves than previously, and try to rebel against what has been accepted before. As this group reaches maturity, Rock 'n' Roll develops with them, in the late '50s and early '60s.

1941 – 1956: Neptune changes signs, into Libra; Pluto is still in Leo. Those born now are more interested in themselves and their relationships than in anything else. Traditional values are overturned and replaced with more liberal, 'softer' views. This is the generation of the hippy philosophy, and the most representative music of the era is that of the Beatles and their contemporaries.

1956 – 1971: Pluto and Neptune both change signs. The new generation has much sharper values, and a streak of cruelty and ruthlessness which can be destructive. Money and power replace emotional satisfaction as the guiding ambition. This generation, currently in its twenties and early thirties, has produced the 'yuppie' philosophy of money and status.

1971 – 1984: Pluto and Neptune enter Libra and Sagittarius. This is a softer generation than its predecessor, with a concern for the future rather than just for the present. Religious values are important to this group, too. At the moment they are mostly at school, but will come to prominence as the next century opens.

1984 on: Pluto and Neptune enter Scorpio and Capricorn. The plans of the previous generation become reality here; this group is far more constructive, and commercially minded, than their predecessors, but not as harsh as the '56 – '71 generation. Great reforms in international politics and financing will take place when this generation, currently small children, grows to maturity.

As Uranus changes signs more frequently than the slower pair of Neptune and Pluto, you can use it to mark off different sub-sections within the generations. Sometimes just a difference of a single year in dates of birth can make all the difference between the values and beliefs of two people from similar background, or even from the same family. Try it and see!

SAGITTARIUS QUICK FACTS

Best Qualities: Intelligence
Optimism
Honesty

Worst Qualities: Carelessness
Tactlessness
Trusting to luck

Best Match: Libra

Worst Match: Capricorn

Favourite Weakness: Travelling

Best Day: Thursday

Worst Day: Saturday

Lucky Numbers: 9, 4, 3

Colour: Deep blue, purple

Birthstone: Amethyst, zircon

Tree: Oak

Flowers: Dandelions, violet

Spices: Cloves, nutmeg

Metals: Tin, pewter

POSTSCRIPT

If you enjoyed finding out about your Sagittarian lifestyle, your relationships, and your appearance, and you would like to go a little deeper into yourself, you might like to read the Sagittarius *Sun Sign Guide*, also from the Aquarian Press. It shows you yourself from the inside rather than the outside, and explains *why* you act the way you do, what you're aiming for, how you handle other people, and how they handle you. It also explains why the zodiac has twelve signs, and how you fit into it all: a book with not just the answers, but the reasons as well.

AQUARIAN SUN SIGN GUIDES

22 NOVEMBER- 21 DECEMBER

Bernard Fitzwalter